S0-EHY-331

Zoom in on
TOPOGRAPHIC
MAPS

Kathy Furgang

E **Enslow Publishing**
101 W. 23rd Street
Suite 240
New York, NY 10011
USA

enslow.com

WORDS TO KNOW

compass rose A symbol on a map that shows direction.

contour lines Lines on a topographic map that show areas with the same elevation.

dimensions The length, width, or height of an object.

elevation Height.

index contours The major contour lines on a topographic map.

intermediate contours The smaller contour lines on a topographic map.

intervals Areas of equal space between two contour lines.

legend A tool on a map that explains what the symbols on the map mean.

ratio The way a size difference between two objects is shown.

scale A tool on a map that compares the length on the map to the length in the real world.

stereoscope An instrument used in mapmaking.

topographic Showing the height or depth of features.

CONTENTS

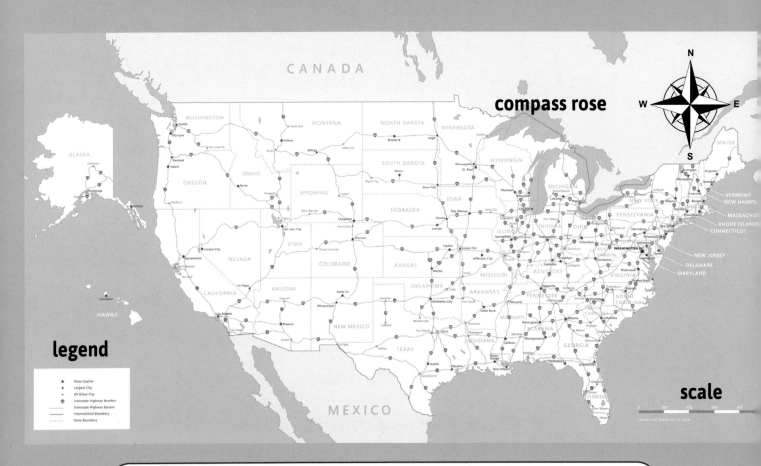

compass rose

legend

scale

On a map, the compass rose shows direction, the scale shows distance, and the legend explains the symbols on the map.

Looking at Maps

There's a lot we can learn from maps. Some tell us how to get from one place to another. Others tell us the locations of different cities and states. Others tell us what the land in an area is like.

Map Tools

Although maps can be different, most of them have three things in common. A legend tells the meaning of the symbols

Hot Spot

The equator is more than just a latitude line that splits Earth between northern and southern hemispheres. It is also the part of Earth that spins closest to the sun, no matter what season it is. This makes the equator the warmest place on Earth.

on the map. A scale tells you how distances on the map compare with distances in the real world. For example, 1 inch (2.5 centimeters) on a map may equal 20 miles (32 kilometers) in the real world. Finally, a compass rose shows where north, south, east, and west are located. This book will teach you about topographic maps.

Lines Like a Grid

Maps have lines on them to help you locate places on Earth. These lines

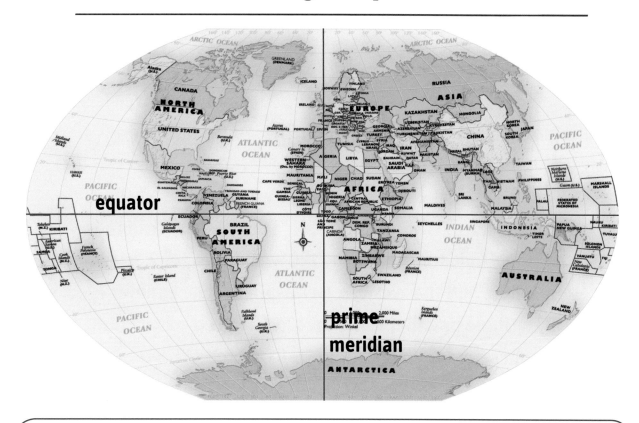

A world map shows longitude and latitude lines. The prime meridian is at 0° longitude, and the equator is at 0° latitude.

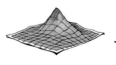

are called longitude and latitude. The distance between these lines is measured in degrees (°). When you have longitude and latitude measurements, you can find the exact location of a place.

Longitude lines run from north to south. Latitude lines run across Earth from east to west. The prime meridian is the 0° longitude line that splits the world into the Eastern Hemisphere and the Western Hemisphere. The equator is the 0° latitude line that splits the world into the Northern Hemisphere and the Southern Hemisphere.

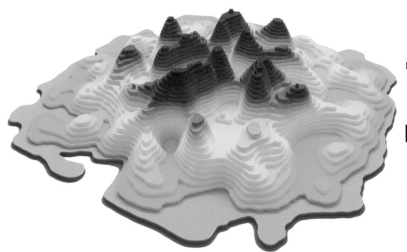

Understanding Topographic Maps

All of Earth's features, such as mountains and canyons, have three dimensions: length, width, and height. Width is the distance between the two length sides. Height is the distance from the bottom to the top. A topographic map shows us the dimensions of Earth's features. So, a topographic map can show how high a mountain is or how deep a lake is.

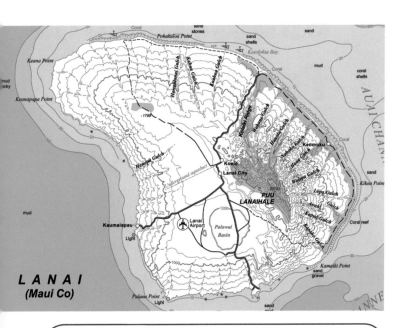

The lines on this topographic map of Hawaii show the different heights of the land. Lanai is one of the Hawaiian islands.

Once you become familiar with how topographic maps work, you can use them to learn new things about the world around you.

Using a Scale

Topographic maps use the same type of measurement for each distance. For example, a topographic scale may show that 1 inch (2.5 cm) on the map

Understanding Topographic Maps

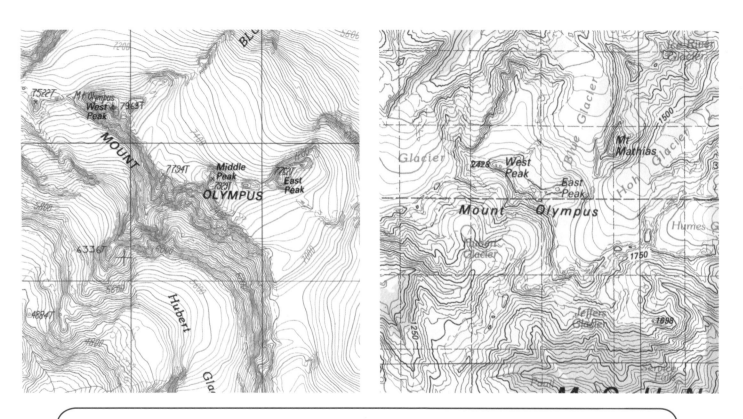

Two topographic maps of Mount Olympus, in Washington State. The map on the left has a ratio of 1:24,000 (1 inch on the map equals 24,000 inches in the real world). The map on the right has a ratio of 1:100,000. That means the map on the left has a larger scale than the right one.

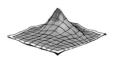

is equal to 63,360 inches (160,934 cm) in real life. That's a distance of one mile! So, the scale is telling you that one inch on the map is equal to one mile in the real world. On a topographic map, this is usually written as a ratio, or relation between numbers. This ratio is written as 1:63,360.

On a map of a large area, such as a country, the scale is a very small ratio. On a map of a smaller areas, such as neighborhoods, the scale is a larger ratio.

Which Unit?

In the United States, large distances are measured in units called miles. In other countries, measurements are made in units called kilometers. It is important to check whether the scale of the map you are using is in miles or kilometers.

Understanding Topographic Maps

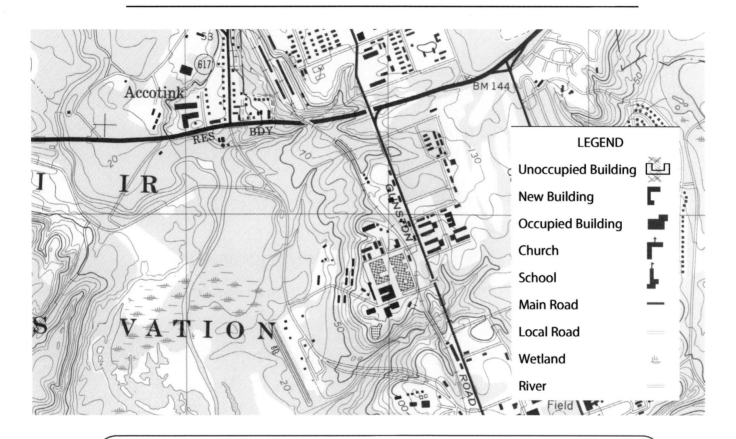

LEGEND

Unoccupied Building	
New Building	
Occupied Building	
Church	
School	
Main Road	
Local Road	
Wetland	
River	

Topographic maps are not just used for land. This map of Fort Belvoir, Virginia, includes things like schools, roads, and bodies of water. The legend explains the symbols for each one.

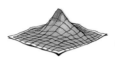

How to Read a Topographic Map

The first thing you'll notice when you look at a topographic map are lots of colorful symbols and lines. Look on the legend to find out what these symbols stand for. You will usually find three kinds of symbols on a topographic map. Point symbols stand for small fixed points, such as schools or hospitals. Area symbols stand for larger areas, such as forests. Line symbols stand for things such as roads.

The legend also color codes the features on the map. Roads can be black or red lines. Red lines show major roads, like highways. Black lines show smaller roads. Bodies of water, like lakes, bays, and rivers, are blue. Forests are green, and just about any human-made object is black.

A World of Contours

How can a map show the dimensions of landforms? Topographic maps use contour lines to show the differences in the land. Each contour line is a group of connected points on the map that are at the same elevation.

Picture a mountain in your mind. Now imagine drawing rings around the mountain, going from the bottom of the mountain to the top. Each ring shows a different height. Now imagine flattening the mountain, so that all you can see are

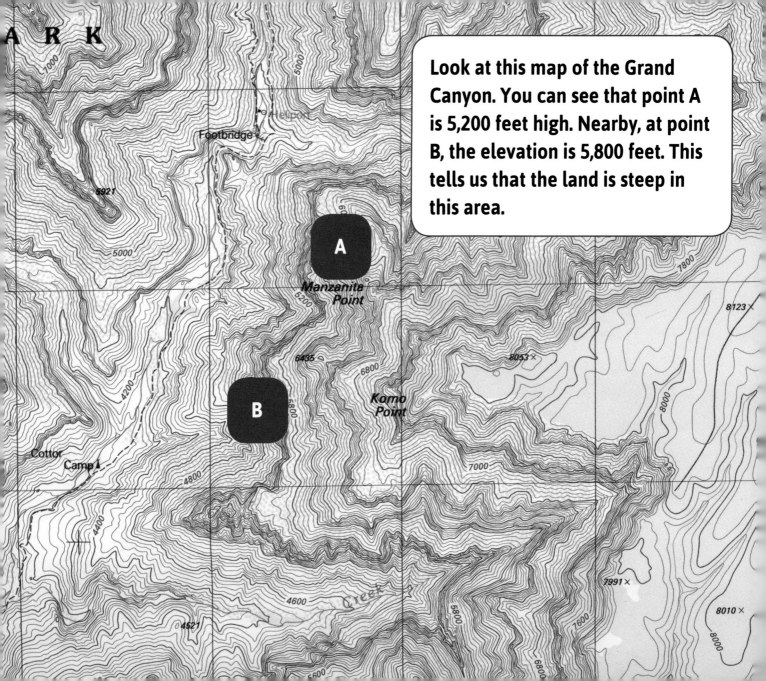

Look at this map of the Grand Canyon. You can see that point A is 5,200 feet high. Nearby, at point B, the elevation is 5,800 feet. This tells us that the land is steep in this area.

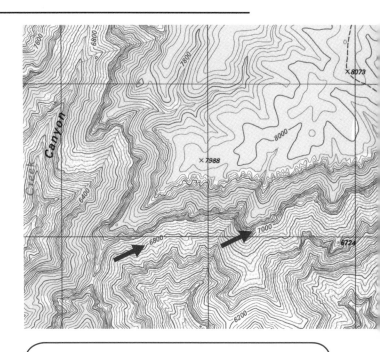

the rings you have drawn. These are the contour lines.

All Kinds of Contours

Each contour line tells you something about the mapped area. Contour lines can be drawn in different shades of brown. There are two main types of contour lines. Index contours are thicker, dark lines that are labeled with a number. This number is the elevation of that contour line.

In another part of the Grand Canyon, thick brown lines show index contours. The arrows point to areas at 6,800 feet and 7,000 feet. The lighter brown lines show intermediate contours.

17

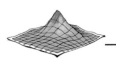

In between index contours are thinner, lighter contours called intermediate contours. Intermediate contours are spaced between the index contours by intervals.

You can tell if the elevation between the contour lines is rising or falling by looking at the difference in the index contours. If the index contour numbers go up, the elevation is rising. If the index contour numbers go down, the elevation is falling.

Deep Sea Mapping

Some maps show the contour lines and topographic features of the ocean floor. The index contour lines and numbers beneath the ocean are shown in different colors than on land.

Using Topographic Maps

There are several uses for topographic maps. Miners and soldiers use topographic maps to understand the landscape. Builders also use topographic maps. For example, suppose a building company wants to make a road between two cities. They would use topographic maps to find out what the land is like. They would use measurements that tell the steepness of the land. This can help them choose the flattest areas to build on. A road that cuts through flatter areas is safer than one that runs through steeper areas.

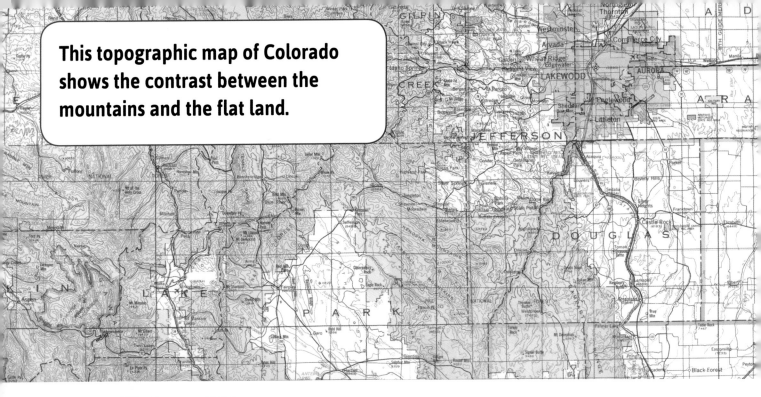

This topographic map of Colorado shows the contrast between the mountains and the flat land.

Take a Hike

Planning a camping trip? A topographic map can be helpful for hikers and campers. It lets people know which areas of a trail or campground are steeper than others. By knowing more about the land, hikers can have a better idea of how long the hike will take. Also, steeper areas can be more dangerous for hikers.

Early Maps

The first topographic map was made in 1879 by the United States Geological Survey (USGS). They made it by measuring the land on foot, which was hard. Since that time many improvements have been made. Today topographic maps are made by taking pictures from airplanes. Mapmakers also use an instrument called a stereoscope to measure the elevation of the land. The USGS has mapped every part of the United States.

Cool Tool

A stereoscope takes photos of the same object at slightly different angles. When the photos are viewed together, the object looks like it has depth.

ACTIVITY: MAKE YOUR OWN MAP

Now that you've learned all about topographic maps, it's time to make a simple one of your own! You will need:

- lump of clay or Play-Doh
- piece of cardboard
- plastic knife
- piece of paper
- pencil

1. On the cardboard, create a clay mountain shape about 4 to 5 inches high. (It can be a little lopsided – that will make your map more interesting!)

2. With the plastic knife, carefully make a mark on your "mountain" about an inch from the top. Make another mark about an inch below that. Keep going until you've divided up your clay into 4 or 5 sections.

3. Use a pencil to poke a hole at the top of the mountain. Push the pencil all the way down until it reaches the cardboard. Then make another hole next to the first, again making sure it reaches all the way down.

4. Use your knife to carefully slice off the top of your mountain where you made the first mark. Place the slice on a piece of paper. Trace around it with a pencil, then put the pencil in one of the holes and make a mark with it. Do the same with the other hole. Move the piece of clay out of the way.

5. Slice off the second top section of the mountain. Place it on top of the tracing you just made. Make sure the two holes in the clay line up with the marks on the paper. Trace around the slice of clay.

6. Repeat for each slice of clay until you have traced all of them. Now you have your own topographic map! Can you see how the map shows which parts of your mountain were steepest? (They will be the lines that are closest together.)

LEARN MORE

Books

Balkan, Gabrielle. *The 50 States: Explore the U.S.A. with 50 Fact-filled Maps!* New York, NY: Wide-Eyed Editions, 2015.

Mizielinska, Aleksandra, and Daniel Mizielinski. *Maps.* Somerville, MA: Big Picture Press, 2013.

Smithsonian Children's Illustrated Atlas. London, UK: Dorling Kindersley, 2016.

Websites

BrainPop Jr.
jr.brainpop.com/socialstudies/geography/readingmaps/
Play games and take quizzes as you learn to read maps.

National Geographic Kids Atlases
www.nationalgeographic.com/kids-world-atlas/maps.html
Learn about different types of maps by exploring them interactively.

INDEX

Published in 2018 by Enslow Publishing, LLC.
101 W. 23rd Street, Suite 240, New York, NY 10011

Library of Congress Cataloging-in-Publication Data
Names: Furgang, Kathy, author.
Title: Zoom in on topographic maps / Kathy Furgang.
Description: New York, NY : Enslow Publishing, LLC, 2018. | Series: Zoom in on maps | Includes bibliographical references and index. | Audience: K to Grade 3.
Identifiers: LCCN 2017018944| ISBN 9780766092211 (library bound) | ISBN 9780766094260 (pbk.) | ISBN 9780766094277 (6 pack)
Subjects: LCSH: Topographic maps—Juvenile literature. | Map reading—Juvenile literature.
Classification: LCC GA130 .F88 2018 | DDC 912.01/4—dc23
LC record available at https://lccn.loc.gov/2017018944

Printed in China

Portions of this book originally appeared in *Topographic Maps* by Ian F. Mahaney.

Photos Credits: Cover, p. 1 ziggymaj/E+/Getty Images; cover, p. 1 (background) pop_jop/DigitalVision Vectors/Getty Images; pp. 2, 3, 22, 23, back cover Login/Shutterstock.com; p. 4 © iStockphoto.com/shoo_arts; pp. 5, 9, 15, 19 ktsdesign/Shutterstock.com; p. 6, 8, 10, 12, 14, 18 PavelNossar/Shutterstock.com; p. 7 Globe Turner, LLC/Getty Images; p. 10 (map) Nadezhda Kochegarova/Alamy Stock Photo; pp. 11, 13, 16, 17 20 United States Geological Survey.

5